Diary of an '80s
Computer Geek

A Decade of Micro Computers,
Video Games & Cassette Tape

By Steven Howlett

Dedications

To Mum

The only unconditional constant in a chaotic universe.

To Darryl Still

Thank you for my first big break.

Twenty years from now you will be more disappointed by the things that you didn't do than by the ones you did. So throw off the bowlines, Sail away from the safe harbour. Catch the trade winds in your sails. Explore, Dream, Discover.

Mark Twain

Introduction

From bright colours and big hair to synthesized songs and day-glo wardrobes. The 80s were certainly loud, often garish and utterly fabulous - no matter how embarrassing the outfits were.

There are so many elements, which made the '80s a truly great decade, but for me personally, one of the greatest contributions, if not the greatest, is the mass introduction of affordable 8-bit home micro computers.

These curious machines of geekdom changed the way we regarded computers and technology. No longer were they the sole pursuit of tweed jacket clad scientists sporting unruly beards, micro computers were now forming a staple inventory in millions of homes.

Much of the technology that we enjoy today, such as desktop computers, notebooks, tablets, gaming consoles and smart phones, all of which are often taken for granted, can be traced back to this innovative decade.

If you were a child of the '80s and remember the joy of receiving your very first home computer or maybe a young adult who fondly remembers the excitement, then you will appreciate this unabashed reminiscence of a simpler time whose adolescent technological was on the cusp of great advancements.

This book is intended as a celebration and reflection of all the computer technology that made the '80s such a wonderful, pioneering period and follows the journey of a self confessed, teenaged computer geek who experienced and enjoyed every ground breaking moment including publishing his own software.

```
10 PRINT "The '80s are fab!"
20 GOTO 10
RUN
```

Chapter 1
Electric Dreams
(or Chapter 00000001 for geeks)

1982 – The UK is at war with Argentina following a long standing dispute over the sovereignty of the Falkland Islands. The Irish based DeLorean Motor Company goes into receivership and Michael Jackson releases the album "Thriller", which is the biggest selling album of all time. Meanwhile, the Commodore 64 and Sinclair ZX Spectrum home computers go on sale for the first time to an unsuspecting public and are an instant hit. In particular, the Commodore 64 eventually sells an estimated 17 million units around the world making it the most successfully selling computer model of all time.

Dear Reader, thank you. Thank you for possessing a keen curiosity, which has encouraged you to join me – a thirteen year old boy - as we together embark on a journey through the exciting 80s. You should also be congratulated on possessing a fine sense of taste by choosing to read this book. Well done you.

Before we begin I think it's important that we establish some important ground rules. Firstly, I am not a geek. Honestly, I'm really not. I don't even know what a geek is, although I suspect it involves a penchant for gizmos, gadgets and snazzy technology? In which case, I can dismiss such foolish thoughts by confirming that I don't posses any technology of any sort. For example, our humble family television set, which pulsates and whines like a mini nuclear power station, has just three part-time channels to choose from, all of which are utter bilge. I don't even own a calculator or digital watch. My life is simple, uncomplicated and that suits me just fine.

Secondly and most importantly, throughout this book I will express my opinions, some of which, wait for it – you may disagree with. The inhumanity of it all! Before you burst a blood vessel, which would be rather messy and detrimental to your health, please consider that it's okay to have varied views and opinions. Imagine a world were everyone wore beige coloured clothes, ate the same food and listened to the same music? Oh yes, that was the Seventies. So now that we have cleared that all up, sit back and let's start this day-glo coloured, synthesized sounding adventure that is the 80s.

Where to start? Well, as I have already mentioned I'm a typical thirteen year old teenager, who begrudgingly attends secondary school during the week and seeks adventure during the weekends. Although the many adventures invariably develop into harmless light-hearted mischief. At this early stage of my young life I have barely began to consider what sort of career I might wish to pursue when I eventually finish school, which at the moment seems like a gazillion light years away. Oh wait, "Light years away", sounds uncomfortably geeky to me.

Let's change that to simply read: "years away". Yeah, that's much better.

At a younger age, I was interested in drawing and painting. After all, what kid isn't? For a short time, a career as an artist seemed desirable, although I wasn't entirely convinced. Eventually as I've grown up the painful realisation has dawned upon me that stick figure style drawing won't cut it in the real world and that I'm very, very crap. It is clear that I will have to consider another career path.

Cooking is fun, sort of. Mother, on occasions has demonstrated the finer art of opening a tin of baked beans and once heated, has artistically draped the contents across a bed of charred bread. However, in these unenlightened times, cooking is considered to be the natural pursuit of women. Television shows in particular are the main culprits for propagating this unfair belief. I told you the three main TV channels were bilge. As a result of this chauvinistic view, cooking lessons are not available to young boys in secondary school. However, good news if you want to act all macho and learn how to build a house or a wall or something equally testosterone based as there are metal, wood or brick building classes. Sadly, if you want to learn how to construct a Battenberg, then you have to ask your Mum, Aunt, Sister or any other female, but not Gran as she has a big, hairy mole on the right hand side of her face, which I'm certain has winked to me on occasions and frankly scares the heck out of me. Ask whomever you like for help, just as long as it's not a big butch bloke.

Unconvinced about the viability of cooking as a career path, I decide to park that conundrum for another day. I have far too many daring escapades to consider and embark upon for the moment. Tally ho!

One day, whilst glancing at a television commercial for a lame-ass national newspaper, I notice it is giving away a free magazine supplement with every purchase. The magazine is all about computers. I am vaguely aware of the term computers. I have witnessed them assist Batman in his Batcave and also help Captain Kirk command the Starship Enterprise. I even recall the large computer cabinets with the big spools of rotating tape during the opening sequence of the Six Million Dollar Man, but ultimately to me a computer is just a big, confusing, box with flashing lights.

Out of curiosity, I visit my local shop and buy the newspaper, which I instantly discard and instead focus on the magazine supplement about computers. The magazine is utterly absorbing. Unbeknownst to me, computers are not just the fanciful conventions of cheesy sci-fi shows, they are actually real. Sorry Trekkies for calling your show cheesy, but remember the grounds rules we discussed earlier?

The magazine features in-depth articles about the popular computers that are currently on the market. The names of the computers are as invocative as their appearances, with thought provoking monikers such as: Acorn Atom, BBC Micro, Dragon 32, Jupiter Ace, Commodore 64, Sinclair Spectrum and ZX81. Next to each entry are large, colourful pictures of weird and wonderful looking devices similar in appearance to typewriters, but not quite the same. Each picture is accompanied with complex technical specifications about processers, RAM and ROMs.

Where had all these computers suddenly come from and what do all those strange and exotic words mean? There are so many different makes and models. This is gripping stuff. I read every word from cover to cover, again and again.

I don't quite understand why I would need a computer, or what I will even do with one, but right now I'm like an obsessed magpie mesmerised by bright shinny objects. In particular, my imagination is fuelled by the concept that regular people can have computers in their homes. Even I could have one. Wow!

My mind races with so many questions foremost of which is how can I learn more about this interesting subject? At this early stage, my secondary school does not have computers on its curriculum and certainly none of my friends own a computer. The modest money I earn through my paper round definitely will not stretch to the cost of a computer so that isn't an option either. I don't think I'm quite brave enough (or capable) to rob a bank. Jeez poverty really does suck.

With my curiosity peaked, I vow to go in search of more information about these marvellous machines. So carry on fair reader, carry on. Let's pick up the pace and see what wonders await us in 1983.

The Battenberg will have to wait.

Chapter 2
Like A Virgin
(or Chapter 00000010 for geeks)

1983 - Whilst saving the galaxy from hoards of evil Stormtroopers, Luke Skywalker learns that his arch nemesis Darth Vader is actually his father. Meanwhile in another galaxy far away, American president Ronald Reagan is devising his own real life version of Star Wars in the guise of the Strategic Defence Initiative (a sort of lasers in space). And in another empire, the Nintendo Famicom Games Console goes on sale in Japan (later known as the Nintendo Entertainment System or NES).

Welcome to 1983 and thank you for remaining with me on my odyssey through the decade. You have joined me in my maths class, which is easily my least favourite subject in school. In fact, I will elaborate even further by stating that I absolutely, positively, 100%, hate maths. Most geeks get some perverse pleasure from the subject. Their highly developed brains allow them to see patterns in the monotonous, complex formulas. I just see numbers, hard work, pain and sheer misery.

To his credit, Mr James always attempts to instil a sense of joviality to his maths classes, but even the affable "Jamesy" cannot detract from the fact that maths makes me weep in despair and my brain hurt. It has on occasion even made my nose bleed. Ok, so I am maybe slightly exaggerating about the nose bleeding, but I just want to give you a clear impression of how much I despise maths.

One day, at the start of what would surely be yet another mundane maths class; everything changes. Jamesy appears from behind the storage cupboard pushing a large trolley, atop of which sits a large, rectangular, device called a BBC Microcomputer. It is the first time I see a real computer.

I sit open mouthed at my first exposure to this exciting, new technology. I am giddy with excitement. The image of this enigmatic machine will be permanently etched on the rear of my retinas. I have found my calling in life. This maths lesson is going to be very interesting.

At this stage lets temporally pause this '80s fuelled trek through Geeksville and switch from maths to history to provide some much needed historical context. Microcomputers were first introduced in 1977 and predominately aimed at the "enthusiastic hobbyists", which is a kinder way of describing nerds, a not too distant relation to geeks, but are less sociably developed. You may have seen the type, almost universally male, window licking, greasy complexion and absolutely no contact with the opposite sex.

They were often sold in kit form, (the computers not the nerds), meaning the consumer would incredulously have to construct their prized possession before they could actually start using it. They were also incredibly expensive with a typical computer kit costing around £500, although there was one notable exception from the kit norm, which was the popular Apple II.

It wasn't until the early '80s when micro computers were mass marketed as affordable and multi functional devices aimed at all the family, although the common use was playing video games. To save on costs, these devices were equipped with an RF modulator, which meant that you could easily connect them directly to a standard television set for image and sound output. The possibilities were seemingly endless and they were an instant success. It was very much a case of computers for the masses, rather than the classes.

The early boom saw an explosion of manufacturers and models hit the scene in a multitude of shapes, colours and specifications, but the early, clear dominators of this fledging market were the Commodore 64 in America and the Sinclair ZX Spectrum in Great Britain and Europe.

It's easy to understand why the Commodore 64 (nicknamed Commie) and the Sinclair ZX Spectrum (nicknamed Speccy) were so popular with enthusiasts over the many other computers. Both were released very early in the boom period and offered a desirable level of specification and functionality for their respected prices. The Commodore 64 cost £229 and featured 64K RAM, 16 colours and 3 voice sound output. Whilst the Sinclair ZX Spectrum cost £125 for the 16K RAM version and £175 for the 48K RAM version, both of which included 8 colours (although it did have a further 8 colours using the 'Bright' mode), and 1 voice sound output.

Very soon, ownership of computers became status symbols amongst the school yard. Children who possessed a Commodore 64 or Sinclair ZX Spectrum were revered as the "cool kids", although infighting between these classes still occurred. Children who had been sadly (and foolishly) supplied with any other computers were labelled as outcasts and ridiculed. The school yard could be a cruel and unforgiving place at times.

Everyone maliciously mocked the kids who owned unpopular machines, such as the Mattel Aquarius with it's poorly placed reset key that users could accidentally strike while programming, wiping out hours of work. The Atari 400 with its completely flat keyboard, devoid of tactile response; that users could not physically tell if they had successfully pressed a key. Then there was the Sord M5, whose namesake had appeared as a deranged computer on a 1960s episode of Star Trek. We had a lot of fun teasing the unfortunate kids who owned that one. Unlucky suckers!

Despite the diversity, children choose to focus on any superficial technological blemish, with which they could then use to propagate the continued, futile argument that their choice of computer was the best.

Okay, so that's enough historic context, let's return back to Jamesy's inane Maths class. I'm about to get my first taste of 8-bit computing. Unfortunately I have to share the experience with 25 other classmates. In a lesson lasting just 45 minutes that potentially means there are only 1.8 minutes with the machine per child. (See! I can do maths; I just don't like doing maths). I don't care. At this early stage I am simply content to be sharing a room with this machine, attentively absorbing every facet, every nuance, every sound emanating from its magnolia coloured shell. Jamesy loads a game from audio cassette called Centipede and each class member enjoys a brief turn playing the game. The exposure to the technology is all too fleeting and I would soon crave more.

In the run up to Christmas this year, Mum asks my brother Mark and me what we would like for our main present. As teenagers, Mum had previously learnt that it was unwise to buy us surprise Christmas presents. Advertising and media pressure gave children a very clear sense of what they wanted and without hesitation, top of our wish list this year is a computer. Ideally, our choice of computer is the Sinclair Spectrum 48K, but the price is too prohibitive for our family. A more feasible option is the affordable, but sadly aging Sinclair ZX81 with just a measly 1K of memory, no sound or colour for only £50. The school yard bullies are about to get new victims!

My parents' marriage had broken down a few years earlier and my Father had departed the scene. Nevertheless, Mum acting as a sole parent with a limited income always does her best to oblige. The early eighties are not exactly an affluent period in Britain and even less so for single parents. So Mark and I feel incredibly fortunate to be given a computer, any computer, at the age of just 14. At the risk of incurring the often vicious school yard snobbery and becoming social pariahs, we graciously accept the offer of a Sinclair ZX81 and look forward to the big day.

The Sinclair ZX81 is a great, low cost induction to this exciting new technology and I will be forever grateful to my Mother for this important start to my career. I can't begin to imagine the sacrifices she had to make in order to save the money for this wonderful gift.

With just 1K of RAM, the ZX81 has the smallest amount of useable RAM of all the computers on the market. This minuscule amount of RAM means that the user can type approximately 24 vertical lines of code, which is roughly equivalent to the vertical height on a domestic analogue TV screen. So 1K is roughly equally to one TV screen of text. 16K is roughly equal to sixteen TV screens of text and so on. Once this limit has been reached the computer will run out of memory and the cursor will blink into nothingness, thus rendering the unceremonious end of all further activity between human and machine.

Thankfully, recognising this technological limitation, Sinclair is now shipping the ZX81 with a separate 16K RAM Pack unit. About the size of a pack of playing cards, this unit can be simply plugged into the back of the ZX81 (always whilst switched off) and will instantly increase the 1K RAM to a more respectable 16K RAM, which will allow the user to enter about 380 lines of code. I can not imagine a situation where anyone would need more RAM than that, ever.

When Christmas finally arrives, my brother and I do what all teenage boys do when given a new home computer, which is to play video games. Software and games are stored on audio cassette tape, which provides the home computer user with a cheap medium to both load and save data. The disadvantages with this medium however are that the software has to be loaded by playing the cassette tape through a cassette player at normal speed, whilst connected to the computer via an audio lead. Loading times vary depending on the size of the program, but a typical loading time for an average commercial game is about five minutes. Cassette tape is also incredible flimsy and prone to degradation and snapping over time or through prolonged use.

The first video game I play on my ZX81 during the Christmas holidays is 3D Monster Maze by a company called J.K. Greye Software. The premise is a simple one. In this first person perspective game (possibly the first of its type), the player is randomly placed within a large maze and the objective is to find the exit. However, the maze is inhabited by a Tyrannosaurus Rex who will try to find you and ultimately eat you. The computer graphics are quite blocky and unrefined, but the image of the large 3D dinosaur suddenly chasing me through the maze is convincing enough for me to shit my pants in terror.

Aside from playing video games it is also possible to program the computer through it's built in language called 'ZX BASIC', which stands for 'Beginner's All purpose Symbolic Instruction Code'.

Here is an example program code listing of ZX BASIC:

```
10 PRINT "WOULD YOU LIKE ME TO TELL YOU A JOKE? (Y
OR N)"
20 INPUT A$
30 IF A$="N" THEN GOTO 200
40 PRINT "HOW MANY EARS HAS MR SPOCK GOT?"
50 INPUT EARS
60 IF EARS=3 THEN GOTO 100
70 PRINT "NO, THE ANSWER IS 3. THE LEFT EAR, THE
RIGHT EAR AND THE FINAL FRONTIER."
80 STOP
100 PRINT "YES. SHALL I TELL YOU IT AGAIN?"
110 GOTO 20
200 PRINT "OKAY, GOOD BYE."
```

Being a 50% owner of the ZX81, with my brother owning the other 50% we take equal turns on using the computer. I am frustrated that I do not have exclusivity with the machine because I want to experiment and learn how to program it. Mark just wants to play games, typically driving games.

One day, whilst Mark is out I pick up the ZX81 owner's manual and learn how to code my first program. It isn't particularly complicated; I just write a few lines of code to move some computer graphics around the screen. I am surprised at how easy it is to do this, or perhaps I simply have an aptitude for coding. Later, when my brother sees what I have done even he is impressed that I have managed to make the machine do something other than play a video game. Is this the start of a passion that will last for many years?

After just a few short weeks, my interest in programming has grown significantly and I develop an appetite to learn much more. I do this by typing in the program code (often referred to as "listings") printed in computer books and magazines and studying each line entry of code. Programming a ZX81 is a tedious, laborious process. This is because the ZX81 has a flat membrane style keyboard, which is not very responsive and means the owner has to apply a certain amount of pressure for every key press. It is a necessary evil in order to continue learning.

Computer magazines often publish the program code listing of games written by other readers for you to copy and type into your computer. Even though it is a tedious and laborious exercise, for the cheap price of a magazine you potentially get a new game for your computer.

One day, whilst visiting my neighbour Alan, we notice an interesting looking ZX81 program listing in a magazine and both agree that we will share the chore of typing it into my ZX81. Alan shares my love of computing and owns the mighty Texas TI-99/4A, which as the name suggests is an American built computer. It is also the first domestic computer with a 16-bit processor. The TI-99/4A is an impressive looking machine finished in black and chrome and has a very smooth tactile keyboard. It seems light years away from my humble ZX81. After several painstaking hours of attentive typing we have almost finished copying the program listing into the ZX81 when disaster strikes. Alan's very young and very bombastic son James comes bumbling through the living room door and brushes against the table on which the ZX81 is sat. The resulting nudge creates just enough vibration to cause a microscopic break in the electrical connectivity between the ZX81 and its 16K RAM pack. Like most technology of this period, the ZX81 unceremoniously crashes and hours of painstakingly code entry is lost forever. In hindsight, we should have taken regular breaks from the code entry and saved our progress onto cassette tape. Disheartened, we decide not to attempt another lengthy typing session and never get to see that program run. It is a lesson that neither of us will repeat again.

Very soon, I have learnt enough about Sinclair BASIC to start making my own video games, albeit simplistic ones. My first effort is called 'Ticking Bomb', where the player has to correctly guess which letter of the alphabet will defuse a bomb. If the player does not guess the code after four attempts then the bomb will explode and the game will be over. I am so pleased with my first effort that I send a copy of my game on cassette tape to a popular home computer magazine. They publish the program code in their magazine and I receive £25 for my effort. I spend all the money on computer magazines and chocolate.

Despite not having contributed in anyway to the program, I list Mark as a co-author so he can enjoy the frill of having his name published in a computer magazine. The reason for doing this is because my quest to learn more about programming is starting to monopolise the computer. I feel guilty about this and it is my way of making up for this. Frustratingly, the magazine prints my name as Stephen instead of Steven. This is the first time I receive payment for my work on a computer. The seed is sown and I am as happy as a slinky on an escalator about the premise that people will pay me for my programs.

Back in the school yard, I discover another potential source of income from my passion with computers. Despite the flimsy nature of cassette tapes they do posses two very useful qualities. They are very cheap and easy to copy. A typical game for the ZX81 in the shops costs about £5, which is a lot of money and means that children usually can only afford new games around the time of their birthdays, Christmas or other special occasions. I make a list of all the games I own and offer a discrete service where I will copy the games onto a blank cassette tape and sell them for 50 pence each. Due to the obvious illegal nature of this business I can not exactly stand on a soap box and shout to the masses, but word gets around the school yard easy enough and business is brisk. At least, that is, for a little while.

The problem with copying and selling computer games is that anyone can do it. You just need a good, cheap supply of blank cassette tapes and two cassette recorders, one to play the master and one to record the copy. Most hi-fi stereo systems come with two cassette tape decks as standard. So this means that most children can eventually get in on the act.

All things considered, this introductory year to computers has been very successful. I have owned my first computer, learnt how to program, made my first computer game and sold my first game to a computer magazine. Along the journey, I have even made some money.

There is no doubt in my mind that I want to learn much more and eventually have some form of career in computers.

Chapter 3
Don't You Want Me
(or Chapter 00000011 for geeks)

1984 – After losing their academic positions at Columbia University, a trio of misfit parapsychologists establish a paranormal exterminator service known as "Ghostbusters" at a retired New York City firehouse. Meanwhile, another type of 'Big Apple' namely the Apple Macintosh 128K is the first commercially successful computer to use a Graphical User Interface (GUI). The computer debuts in a now famous television commercial by Alien and Blade Runner director Ridley Scott during the Super Bowl XVIII and costs an estimated $1.5 million dollars.

At the end of the third year in our comprehensive school, it is customary for every pupil to consider which non-core subjects they want to study during their fourth and fifth years. Once the decision has been made, each pupil then has to approach the subject heads and request their approval to join that class. Computers and technology are in their infancy and not yet a compulsory core subject. So unsurprisingly, at the very top of my educational wish list is Computer Science.

Up until this point, my sole exposure to formal computer education has been limited to the occasional maths lesson where Jamesy has wheeled out the BBC Micro on a trolley, which is then perversely ogled at by a large class size of 25 pupils. These rare occasions typically featured Jamesy loading a video game from cassette tape, an act which seemed to last an eternity and is prone to failure due to the unreliability of the flimsy media. Then each class member takes it in turns to play that game for a few short moments. There is very little tuition, but it nevertheless offers pupils invaluable exposure to the subject of micro computers. The thought of joining the Computer Science class and being formally taught how to operate and program a computer is an exciting prospect.

The head of Computer Science is her Royal Highness Mrs Nicola Jones, whose lofty title has given her a self instilled sense of importance. Even though our paths have never crossed and without either of us realising it, Mrs Jones is about to become an instrumental figure in the next stage of my life.

Having just completed the third term exams and finishing top of my class ahead of the lesser mortals, I feel confident enough to visit Mrs Jones and state my case. I am accompanied by three other classmates who have also elected to study Computer Science. We knock on her Majesty's classroom door and await her confirmation to enter.

Wearing my best possible smile and representing the small group, I introduce ourselves to Mrs Jones and explain that we are here to request her permission to join

Computer Science. Mrs Jones' response is immediate, curt and utterly direct.

> **"Computers are not for you."**
> **"You'll find it too difficult."**
> **"Choose a different subject."**

Three short sentences with a devastating delivery, which will probably remain with me for a long time. In the absence of any in-depth, pre-vetting analysis of my academic background and abilities, without any further discussion whatsoever, the mean spirited old hag looked down her bigoted nose and tossed me and my classmates onto the IT scrap heap. The disappointment is crushing.

How could a seemingly professional educator make such a crucial decision in the early development of a young person's education without any evidence to base this decision? Even if she has legitimate concerns about our suitability for the class surely she can proactively use that knowledge to provide additional guidance? Isn't it better to try and fail than to not try at all?

Industry and marketing experts have strived for years to unshackle the pomposity that shrouds the subject of computers and make it affordable and available to all. If seems Mrs Jones just wants to restrict her classes for what she believes are the best (or maybe her favourite) students. I don't think I will ever forgive Mrs Jones or the school for this reprehensible decision. This act will prevent me from gaining the education I so desperately want.

With our tails tucked between our legs, we leave Cruela's classroom and smile haplessly at the hopelessness of the situation. I should protest, but these are the days when school children are seen and absolutely not heard.

The micro computer boom is now accelerating at an incredible pace. Each week I continue to read in the computer media about the latest and greatest machines constantly being developed and marketed to the consumer. The pace of development in this newly emerging industry is relentless. I can sense the importance of staying up-to-date with this new technology and not get left behind.

Sadly, Mrs Jones' actions have consigned me to a further two terms without formal education in this rapidly rising field of study before I can legally leave and join a dedicated college. This is a massive disappointment and a hugely disadvantaging blow to my desire to stay ahead of the learning curve.

My hunger for knowledge continues to grow. With no other options I continue with my self taught programming, albeit on my humble and aging Sinclair ZX81. Soon, I complete my second game called 'Desert Tank'. This game places the player in a military tank, where the objective is to destroy the enemy stronghold by estimating the range and elevation required for the cannon to successfully strike its target. Unlike my previous game, this is my first game where I have included computer graphics. (My previous game simply featured text only).

Once again, I send a copy of my game on cassette tape to a popular computer magazine and they publish the program listing. They pay me another £25 for my efforts. Frustratingly, they once again publish my name as Stephen instead of Steven.

Sales of my illegal software copying in the school yard are starting to decline. Many of my regular customers have ditched their aging Sinclair ZX81s for the latest models, most notably the Commodore 64 and Sinclair ZX Spectrum, both markets I can not cater for. The computer magazines also appear to echo this trend and are starting to heavily concentrate on the latest and popular models. The writing is on the wall for my trusty ZX81.

One of the big movie events of 1985 is Ghostbusters, which is a huge box office success. In this early example of a successful movie and game tie in, the American software company Activision release the official game for all the popular computers. All that is, except the Sinclair ZX81.

Not wishing to be left out and sensing an opportunity to further increase my programming skills, I set upon creating my own unofficial version of the Ghostbusters game for my ZX81. It is a big challenge, partly due to the limited technical abilities of the ZX81 and partly due to my fledgling programming skills. However, after a few hours of coding I have managed to create a reasonable facsimile of part of the official game. Sadly, due to the ZX81's slow processor, the game operates at such a slow pace it is frustratingly unplayable.

This is the first occasion where my imagination has outgrown the technical abilities of my machine and I vow to somehow find a way to upgrade to a newer, more powerful computer. I discuss a cunning plan with my brother, which is to pool our pocket money and ask our mother if we can hire purchase a new computer from her home shopping catalogue. This method allows you to buy goods by paying a fixed amount on a weekly basis, albeit for a slightly inflated price. After a bit of persuasion, Mother agrees to our proposal and all that remains is for us to decide which computer to buy.

The three main contenders at this time are the Commodore 64, The Sinclair Spectrum and the BBC Microcomputer. All three computers are very popular and have a massive following. The later option has the added advantage of being in every school in the UK, but it is also the most expensive of the three. Not wishing to have our pocket money tied up in hire purchase payments for an eternity, we eventually opt to buy the new and improved ZX Spectrum 48K Plus, which as the name suggests has a whopping 48K of RAM. I can not imagine a situation where anyone would need more RAM than that, ever. The computer also features an updated plastic keyboard over the rubber keyboard on the previous models. The price of £175 seems very reasonable. Another factor for our decision is that the computer shops extensively stock software and video games for this machine, again adding further credibility to our belief that this is a popular machine.

For me personally, I have already invested a whole year in learning ZX BASIC and as the ZX Spectrum features the same programming language (albeit with additional commands) I can utilise my existing knowledge and expand on it even further. There are several differences between the ZX BASIC languages on the ZX Spectrum and ZX81. Most noticeably are the additional programming commands for colour, sound and user defined graphics (UDG). These three elements are not available on the Sinclair ZX81 so I will have much to learn and sink my teeth into on the new computer. Mark of course, continues to play games, mostly driving games. He particularly enjoys Chequered Flag by Psion Games and Pole Position by Atarisoft.

At school, I'm now officially a cool kid. With my chest pumped out I proudly and loudly announce to the universe that I'm a ZX Spectrum owner. I'm no longer going to suffer the humiliating stigma of being a ZX81 owner. The ZX Spectrum owning fraternity are quick to welcome me into their guild. The Commodore 64 owners of course have someone new to loath. School yard politics continue to perplex.

With a new computer comes new challenges and I first decide to explore the wonderful world of sound. Unlike the ZX81, the ZX Spectrum has a single channel sound chip with an eight octave range. Compared to the Commodore 64's three channel sound output the ZX Spectrum's sound is rather poor. Nevertheless, I decide to write a program, which mimics a musical instrument and enables the user to play their Spectrum's keyboard as if it were a musical keyboard. I sarcastically name the program Beep Box in honour of the ZX Spectrum's modest sound output.

Disappointing, after a few short weeks, the new ZX Spectrum 48K Plus develops a fault, which means it will have to be returned to the home shopping catalogue. Thankfully, the computer is still well within its twelve month warranty period so it will either be repaired of replaced. Personally, I don't care which; I just hope the computer comes back to me very soon. My programming knowledge of this new machine is still in its infancy and in the absence of formal computer education from my school it's also my solitary source of learning. It's an untimely blow for my education and development.

Sadly, my worst fears are realised when days evolve into weeks and there is still no sign of activity from the home shopping catalogue. I ask mother to intervene and telephone the catalogue to find out when the computer will be returned. Mother obligingly telephones the catalogue, but the news is not good. They explain to my Mother that the new ZX Spectrum 48K Plus has been a very popular computer and that they are experiencing difficulties in getting sufficient supplies from Sinclair. There is more bad news to come. Added to this popularity is the further complication of quality issues with the new computer. So not only are retailers finding it difficult to sell to new customers, but they are struggling to service their existing ones.

The computer media soon confirm the availability and quality issues with Sinclair and their new computer and I'm now a statistic in a rapidly growing tally. In a simple act of resignation I dig in for the long wait, dust off my old ZX81 and enjoy some programming time with my aging friend. Minus colour, sound, user defined graphics, a decent processor and a tactile keyboard. It's curious how these limitations were not a factor a year ago.

In an effort to keep my programming skills sharp I start coding a new game called Bug Race on my ZX81. The game features four racing bugs and invites the player to guess and bet virtual money on which bug will win the race. Bug Race is an entertaining game and easily the best work I have completed to date, but I'm keen to disassociate myself from the ZX81. So unlike my previous games, I decide not to send it to any computer magazines.

I'm still hangover from Mrs Jones' bigotry and the faulty ZX Spectrum. Collectively these two events have dampened my spirits. No matter how hard I try to progress, it feels that their entire universe is conspiring against my thirst for knowledge. Learning opportunities should never be this difficult to access.

Much to my relief, the home shopping catalogue eventually dispatches a replacement ZX Spectrum 48K

Plus and once again I'm readopted back into the ZX Spectrum owning brotherhood. More importantly, I'm once again expanding my knowledge of programming on a superior computer.

Eventually, the day I have long awaited arrives. It's the last day of school. It's a bittersweet moment. I'll be saying goodbye to the friends that I have known for five years, but I will be free to pursue further education through a college in the subjects that I yearned for the last two terms.

When I arrive home from my last day at school, I stick a garden fork in the lawn, take off my school tie and gently drape it on the fork's wooden handle. I then pour a liberal amount of white spirits over the tie and very carefully ignite it. Like an enthusiastic Morris Dancer, I then perform a merry jig around the flaming tie and sing repeatedly "I'm free, I'm free. No more school for me". Mark witnesses the excitement and even though he's still got a further two terms to endure at the same school, he joins in the song and dance routine. Mother soon discovers what we are doing and angrily leans through an open window and barks at us both to put the fire out. Begrudgingly, we comply with the killjoy's request and collapse on the lawn in fits of laughter. Nothing can spoil the moment. In a few weeks time I will be attending a college of further education and studying the subject of my dreams.

And it's not Battenberg.

Chapter 4
Careless Whisper
(or Chapter 00000100 for geeks)

1985 – In an effort to raise much needed funds for relief for the ongoing Ethiopian famine, a musical concert called Live Aid is simultaneously held in the United Kingdom and United States. It is one of the largest-scale satellite link-ups and television broadcasts of all time with an estimated global audience of 2 billion, across 150 nations. Meanwhile the next generation of 16-bit home computers debuts with the release of the Atari ST. It has a huge 512K of RAM and it is also the first home computer to feature built in MIDI ports.

I've finally broken free of the debilitating shackles of my secondary school and have enrolled in a college of further education, where I will be studying computers and technology for the next two years. It's an exciting time. The itinerary reads like a virtual smorgasbord of technological geekdom. Computers, programming and micro electronics all feature extensively on my two year timetable. I will also be amongst students with a similar passion and desire to learn more about these subjects.

Frustratingly, after just a few short weeks, the replacement piece-of-crap ZX Spectrum 48K Plus develops the exact same fault as the original computer and once again has to be returned to the supplier. Unlike the previous occasion, the sense of urgency is lessened due to the availability of computers at the college but I'm still keen to get a replacement as soon as possible. After several weeks, the continued pressure from Mark and me towards our Mother eventually encourages her to contact the home shopping catalogue and press for a speedy resolution. This time our Mother requests a full and immediate refund of balance paid thus far and threatens to close her account with them and take her business elsewhere. The tactic works and the home shopping catalogue offer a compromise. Their proposal is that we take immediate delivery of the new Sinclair ZX Spectrum 128K Plus, but for the cost of the ZX Spectrum 48K Plus. This is great news. The new computer as its name suggests, has a massive 128K RAM. I can not imagine a situation where anyone would need more RAM than that, ever. The computer also boasts a three channel sound output. We would be amongst the first to own this wonderful new model and best of all we would be paying the same price as the 48K model.

Poor Mother, with no understanding of RAM, bits or bytes, in fact, with no computer or technology knowledge whatsoever, simply doesn't realise the benefits of this great offer. Once I explained the situation to her the deal is swiftly agreed, the order processed and one shiny new ZX Spectrum 128K Plus is shipping its way from Sinclair HQ to two very happy teenage boys. Almost overnight, my status will be elevated from a former ZX81 owning ragamuffin to a ZX Spectrum 128K Plus owning deity, but it isn't the kudos that I crave, that is just a happy bi-product of this new world. Like my previous computers, I just want to explore the microscopic universe within its protective plastic shell.

At the college, every Wednesday afternoon, the entire campus participates in sporting activities. I'm not sure how or who had created this initiative, whether it be the local education authority or indeed the college itself, but regardless, it is a welcome break from an intense week of studying. After lunch on each Wednesday, an entourage of buses and coaches assemble at the front of the campus and students board the vehicle that has been assigned to transport them to the venue, which hosts their pre-chosen sporting activity. Most of my group have chosen the region's Leisure Centre. It is a popular venue and caters for a large range of sports. The best part about the Leisure Centre is that it is located next door to a video games arcade, which is packed to the rafters with the latest and greatest video gaming technology

A visit to the video arcade before participating in our sports activity has become part of our Wednesday afternoon ritual. Of course, we all possess home computers, but our 8-bit technology doesn't compare to the mighty processing power of the modern video arcade machines. The video arcade is an exciting, vibrant place to visit. The venue is awash with a sensory overload of colour and noise, hosting classic favourites such as 'Asteroids', 'Defender', 'Pacman' and the all conquering 'Space Invaders'. The video arcade also houses new and exciting games, such as the multiplayer, fantasy themed 'Gauntlet' and the driving game 'Outrun' with it's innovative moving cabinet.

One of our favourite games is a Snooker themed, general knowledge, trivia game called 'Give Us A Break, which offers a cash prize if the player achieves a high score. Each week, about 5 or 6 of us huddle around the quiz machine and use our collective intellect to try and answer the game's trivia questions correctly and win the cash prize.

One particular week, I stare at the machine and begin analysing the game more intently. I start to consider how the game functions. I wonder about the software code that is driving the graphical display and how the questions are being presented to the player in a random format. Then I have an eureka moment. "I can make this game on my computer". I quietly whisper to nobody in particular. The boast is barely loud enough for the group to hear and they immediately respond with several jibes such as "Yeah sure!" and "Stop being silly Steven". It isn't my intention to audibly boast to the group about my programming prowess. I am simply absorbed by the game and lost in the moment. I am surprised at the seemingly simplicity of the game. I genuinely believe that I possess the necessary skill and experience to replicate the game on my home computer. Despite their lack of confidence in my programming abilities I am certain that I have the coding knowledge to convert this game to my home computer format. I do not think there is anything particularly difficult about the game that I can not reproduce on my beloved Speccy at home. We depart the video game arcade (cashless as usual) and go to the Leisure Centre to participate in our designated sporting activities. Throughout the entire afternoon my mind continues to think about the quiz game and without realizing it, I have already started to consider how to code the game.

Later that evening, I sit at my computer desk and stare at the blank empty screen of my new ZX Spectrum 128K Plus. This is possibly the most difficult moment for any programmer. All you have is an idea, a thought and somehow you've got to find a way of translating that thought into a computer programme via a series of lines containing the computer language. I imagine the process is similar to a writer, sat at their word processor when starting to write a book. That initial blank, white empty page is a lonely place to start any creative journey, but unlike the author of a book, the computer programmer can't use plain English words. They have to use the language that the computer understands, making the processes even more challenging.

Since there is no manual, which explains the correct way to start such a project I decide that I will start with the computer graphics. This is always my preferred method of starting any programming project for two reasons. Firstly, I find it quite easy to create computer graphics and possess a competent sense of design. Secondly, once the computer graphics are created and in place you very quickly gain a sense of how good the program will look.

Even though the program does not work at this stage, the static computer graphics affords me a good sense of how the program will appear once complete. It is a good quick win and a perfect dollop of encouragement to continue with the programming project. Later that evening, after many painstaking hours of programming, I finally complete the initial computer graphics for my game. They resemble the video arcade machine closely and I am very satisfied with the results so far.

The next evening, I began the tricky task of coding the main bulk of the program. Creating eye pleasing computer graphics is all well and good, but behind them they will need a clever piece of code to make them move and interact with the player. Programming is a particularly, isolated undertaking. With just the soft glow of the black and white, analogue television, I would often sit alone in my bedroom and become lost in the task. Minutes would very quickly evolve into many hours. To aid my concentration I would often play a vinyl album quietly on the record player. I've recently purchased a-ha's Scoundrel Days, a typical '80s sounding synthpop album. Its uncomplicated, electronic tones are pleasing and seem to facilitate my thought process. The progress of my game is very slow going. This is unquestionably my most ambitious programming project to date. Each night I continue to chip away at the mammoth programming task, code by code, line by line and keep edging one step closer to completion.

In parallel to my evening activities, my college work is progressing very well. One day, our class is given an assignment to write a computer program with an educational theme on the BBC Microcomputer. After some consideration, I decide to convert my previous ZX Spectrum title "Beep Box". The programming language on the BBC Micro is very similar to ZX BASIC. The main principles are almost identical. The ZX Spectrum version is still very fresh in my mind and I am able to convert the program in a very short time.

Unlike the ZX Spectrum version, which simply mimics a music keyboard, the BBC Micro version needs an educational twist to satisfy the parameters of the assignment. In order to overcome this I add a section, which displays music notation of some nursery rhymes and teaches the user to replicate them through the keyboard. It is very simple, but very effective.

Our college computer class is facilitated by two staff members. The main teacher, Mrs Edwards appears completely out of her depth and I question whether she actually has any qualifications or experience in the subject. The second staff member is the Computer Technician whose main responsibility is to ensure the smooth operation of the classroom and its equipment. It is clear from his computing skills that he is easily the brains of the teaching partnership. He also never speaks, ever.

Eventually, I complete my conversion of Beep Box onto the BBC Microcomputer and give a demonstration to Mrs

Edwards and my classmates. The Computer Technician walks by and glances at my program. He stops briefly and speaks for the first time. "Oh, that's good." My classmates are begrudgingly in awe of the praise. The Computer Technician has never spoken to anyone. Now I am being singled out for his praise. At this particular stage in our educational development there is no higher power, no greater praise to be found. I am thrilled by the approval.

Part of my college course requires me to take an active job experience role with a local employer. One day, Mrs Edwards asks me if I have a preference for the type of employer I would like to work with for the week long duration. Having never been in any form of working environment previously I explain to Mrs Edwards that it is difficult for me to answer her question as I do not have any context in which to base an answer. Mrs Edwards, determined to help asks me what sort of activities I enjoy outside of college. I explain to her that I enjoy using computers (obviously) and that I am a fan of video games. On that basis, Mrs Edwards suggests that I might enjoy working at the computer store in the city centre. It doesn't take me long to realise the immediate benefits of such a work placement. If I work in the computer store I will have unlimited access to the latest computers and video games. I quickly agree to the proposition and Mrs Edwards promises to make the necessary arrangements.

A few weeks later, I arrive at the computer store for my week long work experience. Like the local video game arcade, the computer store is always a noisy hub of frenzied activity. All the latest computer makes and models are on display and powered up for potential buyers to try. There are dozens of shelves packed with brightly coloured software boxes for all the popular computer formats. Mrs Edward's suggestion has been a good idea. This was going to be a great work experience.

During my week long work placement, I am fortunate enough to experience the almighty Atari ST, which is a new 16-bit computer from America. The machine is packed with state-of-the-art features including a colossal 512K RAM. I can not imagine a situation where anyone would need more RAM than that, ever. The Atari ST also features a built in disk drive and a mouse. The operating system uses an intuitive Graphical User Interface (GUI), called GEM, which is a far cry from the text based interface used on the majority of the 8-bit computers. The graphic and sound capabilities are incredible. Being a newly released computer there is not a great deal of software available for it at this early stage, but one title that never fails to draw a crowd of slack jawed lollygaggers is Starglider by Argonaut Software. This game really does show off the capabilities of the Atari ST beautifully. The game is a futuristic, 3D first person, combat flight simulator with colourful, rendered, vector graphics. At the game's main title screen there is an impressive 15 second long sound sample featuring synthesizers and a real male voice singing "Starglider... by Rainbird". In comparison to the 8-bit computers, the Atari ST is utterly impressive. Seeing the Starglider game makes me realise that producing games for 16-bit computers was now a team effort rather than the pursuit of a lone individual. The graphic and sound capabilities are so impressive that I envisage a specialist team of people all working together to produce games of this calibre. It is certainly something to be mindful of for the future.

The week long placement in the computer store has given me my first taste of a working environment. From my point of view, the experience has been a worth while endeavour if just to have had the exposure to the new Atari ST. I am grateful for the experience and return back to the college course.

Back in the bedroom, the programming momentum is progressing well on my conversion of the video arcade quiz machine. The coding is relatively straightforward. The hardest part is trying to capture all the various nuances of the video arcade game from memory as I don't have any notes or photographs with which to reference. In a manner of speaking, my brain is acting as a sort of biological interface between the video arcade game and the ZX Spectrum conversion. I like that thought. In total, I take a painstaking six months to complete the game to a standard that I feel is comparable to the video arcade game version. I use up every single available byte of the 48K RAM available to me. Even though I have a new computer capable of 128K RAM, the ZX Spectrum 48K is still the most popular of the ZX Spectrum formats. I decide to limit the size of the game to 48K to ensure compatibility with the majority of ZX Spectrum owners.

During the programming process, I subconsciously learn every word to every song on the Scoundrel Days album.

The programming conversion is exhausting and the entire project has felt like a long drawn out marathon. At the end there is a real sense of achievement. It's an exciting moment when you press the RUN command and press the ENTER key to play a computer game that you have created for the first time.

Every game needs a name and I need to find one worthy for my new masterpiece. The name of the original video arcade game version is 'Give Us A Break'. I want to somehow capture the spirit and feel of that title in my own game, but without infringing on any obvious trademarks or copyrights. After some thought, I decide on the snappy name 'Break Point', which I think ties in nicely with the snooker theme and the premise of the game, which is to acuminate points.

With the programming completed and the new name added to the loading screen all that remains is to proudly show my masterpiece to the world.

I can't wait to demonstrate the game to my doubting classmates.

Chapter 5
Walking On Sunshine
(or Chapter 00000101 for geeks)

1986 – As the world watches live, the NASA Space Shuttle Challenger brakes apart 73 seconds after takeoff and disintegrates over the Atlantic Ocean, leading to the deaths all seven crew members. Meanwhile, Sinclair Research sells its entire computer product range and the 'Sinclair' brand name to rivals Amstrad. The unexpected announcement signals the end of a great British computer innovator and manufacturer.

Armed with a cassette tape and an all knowing wry smile, this Wednesday afternoon is going to be very different from the norm.

In a departure from the usual visit to the video games arcade I have asked my classmates if we can visit the local computer shop instead. Like the video games arcade it is situated near the leisure centre. We won't be able to play any video games, but we can at least look at the computers and software on display. More importantly, the computer shop has a ZX Spectrum for customer's to play with.

It has been six very long, very lonely months since my non intentional boast in the video games arcade and all the usual suspects are assembled in front of the ZX Spectrum in the local computer shop. It is an exciting moment, at least for me. My classmates however, look mildly bemused and their expressions belay a sense of indifference. I insert the cassette tape into the cassette player, type LOAD "" and press the ENTER key. Then we wait. The typical time for a ZX Spectrum game to load from cassette tape is about five minutes, but after about 1-2 minutes the monotony is slightly interrupted by the appearance of a loading screen. The concept is similar to a book cover, where the name of the game and the author is displayed along with a graphic presentation of the game. When the loading screen appears my classmates get their first hint at what they are about to see. Their mood changes quickly to that of inquisitiveness. My wry smile grows slightly wider.

Eventually the loading process completes and Break Point receives its official debut in the tiny corner of the computer shop. I could not be more proud. At this point the reactions from my classmates can be summarised into two categories. One half look at the game with astonishment and quickly wrestle amongst themselves for a turn. The other half feigns a look of indifference, but slyly continues to watch the game being played. I stand silently with my wry smile and bask in the glory. This perfect moment is the accumulation of six long months, all of which was originally triggered by an unguarded murmur.

Mission accomplished. Or so I thought. One of my classmates is about to make a comment, which will set me on a new adventure. "This game is good enough to be released commercially. You should sell it." It had seemed like an obvious statement, but I had become so enthralled with my programming project that it hadn't occurred to me that this was a game worthy of a proper commercial release. It has taken an inconspicuous exhibit in the corner of a local computer shop and a comment from a classmate for the realisation to become apparent.

My classmate was right. This game is good enough to be released commercial. I just need to work out how to do that. Writing a computer program is a challenge in itself, trying to sell the program is a different challenge completely. After some thought, I decide I will attempt to market and sell my game on my own by starting a mail order software business. After all, this is a boom period in the home computer industry and the computer media are continually reporting about small start up companies, whose origins are born from the bedrooms.

One of the important aspects of starting a mail order software business is a trading name. Of course, I could use my name to represent the business, but this is rarely done with computer software. Mostly, software companies and mail order software businesses use snappy trading names and I decide to follow suit. My favourite television show at this time is the American action series 'Airwolf'. The show features a high-tech military helicopter, code named Airwolf, and its crew as they undertake various missions, many involving espionage, with a Cold War theme. I like the name

Airwolf, but obviously due to copyright restrictions I will not be able to use it to represent my mail order software business. Also, a British software company called Elite Systems have previously released a game for all the popular formats called 'Airwolf'. So even if copyright issues could be averted, the existing game and name will complicate matters. A compromise is needed and my eventual chosen mail order software trading name is 'Airline Software'. I like the simplicity and quickly design a logo, which is loosely based on the one used by British software publisher 'Ocean Software'.

With the trading name decided upon, it is time to book an advertisement in the computing press. With a little research, I learn that the best selling ZX Spectrum dedicated magazine at this time is Crash. I will pay for an advertisement and advertise my game directly through the magazine and manufacture and sell the game by mail order from my home. There is a lot of preparation to be done. There is an advert to design, and a cassette inlay to produce. I also need to source a supply of good quality blank cassette tapes. This is a mammoth undertaking, but it is also good fun.

The magazine advertisement costs exactly £200 and I will be advertising the game for £5.99. I will need to sell at least 33 copies of my game to break even and that's without even taking into consideration the costs of production, supplies and postage charges. Nevertheless, Crash Magazine has the biggest readership figure and I am reasonably confident that my advertisement will generate enough interest to cover the initial outlay.

I could not have been more wrong. When the magazine eventually goes on sale, the resulting sales for my game are disastrous. Break Point sells a disappointing six copies. In hindsight it's difficult to learn why the response has been so limited. It could have been the small size or design of the advertisement. It could have been the price point or even the name of the game. I will never know. One thing I do know for sure is that the low interest is not a direct reflection of the game itself. The software buying public can't judge a game they haven't seen or played. I am still confident that I have a reasonably good product and I will find another way to somehow sell my computer game.

An unexpected news item is the announcement from British computer manufacturer Sinclair Research that it needs to raise additional revenue to restructure its company. Despite the enormous popularity and success of the ZX computer range, Sinclair has experienced a series of embarrassing and very expensive failures with several other products and the loss of confidence in the company is proving hard to overcome.

The Sinclair TV80 pocket television, which had been launched in 1983, featured an innovative flattened CRT screen, but it had failed to capture the public's imagination and had only sold 15,000 units. The poor sales didn't even cover its development costs, which were estimated at four million pounds. Another failed product was the Sinclair QL computer. Priced at £399 this 32-bit microcomputer aimed at business and professional users, was hampered by production delays, hardware reliability problems and software bugs. Despite the QL's hugely advanced architecture, its image never recovered from its poor production and reliability problems.

Eventually, Sinclair Research sells its entire computer product range and the "Sinclair" brand name to British rivals Amstrad. This deal does not involve the company, merely its name and products. The British computer industry had been kick started by the drive and ambitions of Sir Clive Sinclair and the ripples of that proverbial boot had been felt across the world. The loss of the once mighty Sinclair Research as a computer innovator and manufacturer marks the beginning of the end of an era. I am particularly sad the see the ZX Spectrum being unceremoniously orphaned off to the highest bidder.

A few weeks later, having healed my wounds from the failed attempt to start a mail order software business, I decide to revisit the subject of how to sell my game. The next obvious step is to approach the software companies and see if they are interested in buying my game from me. I have no idea how to do this. These really are pioneering times. So I decide to simply send copies of my game to a handful of computer software publishers along with covering letters and see if there is any interest.

Laid out on the floor of my bedroom are ten padded envelopes, ten cassette tapes, each with a copy of my game recorded on to them and ten A4 sized letters. I methodically place a letter and cassette into each of the ten envelopes and carefully write the name and address of ten computer software publishers on the front of the padded envelopes. There isn't any real thought process behind the selection of the computer software publishers. I simply choose the companies that I am familiar with and whom have recently been actively releasing computer games for the ZX Spectrum. A quick visit to the local post office and within moments, ten tiny packages of ZX Spectrum software are winging their way across the country to impress whoever will receive and open them. And so the waiting game begins.

An interesting item in the computer media reports that Apple Computer co-founder Steve Jobs has paid 10 million dollars to Lucasfilm to purchase the Special Effects Computer Group. This specialist division of Lucasfilm had previously created computer animated segments of popular films such as the Genesis effect in Star Trek II: The Wrath of Khan and the Stained Glass Knight in Young Sherlock Holmes. Jobs pays $5 million to George Lucas and puts $5 million as capital into the company, which will specialise in high-end computer hardware and sell primarily to government agencies, the medical community and Disney Studios. Jobs renames the company to Pixar. I wonder what the future holds for them.

After a few days, I receive a package through the mail. Without opening the package I can tell that it contains a cassette tape. Since I haven't recently purchased any software by mail order it doesn't take me long to realise that this package probably contains one of my cassette tapes being return to me. I open the package and sure enough I have received my first response from one of the ten computer software publishers. The letter disappointingly explains that they are grateful that I have considered them to review my game for publication, but upon evaluation they conclude that they do not want to pursue my submission any further blah blah blah etc. One down, nine to go.

Not long after, I receive another telltale package, complete with rejection letter. Then another one and then another. The computer software publishers are, if nothing else, very efficient in their rejection process. Eventually, I incredulously receive nine rejections in a very short space of time and even though one remains outstanding I am resigned to the possibility that my game will never see the light of day. Certainly the odds are now stacked against me. The days that follow become a guessing game to see when the postman will deliver the final bulky rejection package through the letterbox.

Then one day, the familiar tell tale rattle of the letter box signals that the postman has delivered his final cruel blow. This time, a simple, ambiguous letter is rested on the floor near the front door. The letter is flat, light and addressed to me. It definitely does not contain one of my cassette tapes being returned. I pluck up the courage to open the envelope and nervously start to read the contents. The letter is from a company called Top Ten

Games and thanks me for sending a copy of my game to them for evaluation. The letter explains that the company are formally requesting my permission to commercially sell my game. Enclosed with the letter is a two page contract, which attempts to explain the financial details of the proposed arrangement. The contract is typically worded in a manner, which the reader requires a law degree to understand it. The complexity of the wording coupled with my frenzied state of euphoria means that I pretty much gloss over the finer details of the contract, but I do note with interest a specific section that explains I will receive something called "royalties", which I understood to be a percentage for each game sold. Holly shit! I had done it. I had bloody done it.

At the tender age of just seventeen and whilst still at college, I am about to become a published software author. In a flurry of excitement I run screaming through the house in search of Mother to share my good fortune. When I eventually find her I can barely get the words out of my mouth fast enough. The scene is amusingly reminiscent of the moment in the movie Willy Wonka's Chocolate Factory, when Charlie Bucket finds a golden ticket hidden in a bar of chocolate. Mother can obviously tell from my frenzied state that this is wonderful news, but I don't think she really understands what the contract means to me and what it could possibly do for my career or indeed my finances. It didn't matter. Together we gaze at the contract and enjoy a perfect moment, the origins of which had been created three years earlier when Mother had given me (and Mark) the ZX81 computer as a Christmas gift.

Back in college, the end of my two year stint is upon me. It's been an incredible time. Unlike my woeful secondary school I have really enjoyed every moment. The subjects, the teachers, the students, the attitudes, everything has been just perfect. Best of all, I received the tuition that had been so unfairly denied me years earlier.

Once I had sat my end of course exams I bid farewell to my college friends and consider what to do with the next stage of my life. My computer game is about to be released commercially in the shops and I will eventually receive some form of payments, but I have been forewarned by the software publisher that this was unlikely to occur for some time. I can continue to write programs at home, but this will not generate any immediate income and Mother will now need some form of financial contribution from me. All things considered, there is no alternative. I will have to get a job, hopefully, one which will somehow involve my love of computers and technology.

Look out world, here I come.

Chapter 6
Manic Monday
(or Chapter 00000110 for geeks)

1987 – Star Trek: The Next Generation debuts on American television and is watched by 27 million viewers. Set roughly 80 years after the original series, the new show features a new crew and a new Starship Enterprise. Meanwhile, Commodore releases the Amiga 500, a new 16-bit computer and the main competitor to the Atari ST. The A500, as it is also known, costs £599 and is superior in almost every area, apart from its MIDI capabilities.

Job hunting is tough. There are so many aspects to consider when browsing through the job vacancies at the Jobcentre. The type of role, employer, salary, working hours, employee benefits, all have to be carefully considered before making any application. Finding a job is almost a job in itself.

College has done a wonderful job in educating me about computers and technology. Unfortunately, aside from a small work experience assignment in a local computer shop, it has ill prepared me for the daunting task of what to do next. Secondary school is now a horrible, cruel, distant nightmare and the euphoria from college education has come to an end.

Whilst perusing the situations vacant of the local newspaper I notice an advertisement for a "Computer Sales Person" in a local department store. I know the store very well and have purchased ZX Spectrum games from there on many occasions. The advisement goes on to explain the role in more detail and lists the responsibilities of the successful applicant, which includes; selling home computers, software and ordering stock. Aside from my ill conceived and short lived pirate software activities in the school yard, I have never sold anything to anyone before, but I am passionately familiar with the subject matter. How difficult can it be? As an eighteen year old who has just completed college this seems a reasonable first step in any career. It will bring in some much needed income and afford me some breathing time whilst I patiently await the outcome of my first computer game being released on to the market. I write to the store and formally apply for the position.

Meanwhile, the software publisher that is about to release my game writes to me to advise that they want to change the name of my game. They explain that they feel my original chosen name 'Break Point' is too closely associated with the sport of Tennis and will complicate their marketing activities and adversely affect sales. The letter goes on to explain that their proposed new name for my game is 'Snookered', which is both a reference to the sport of snooker and also an apt description of someone that is stumped by a difficult question. They also request a slightly modified version of the game, including a new loading screen to reflect the new moniker. It is a clever title for my snooker themed, general knowledge, trivia game. Frustratingly, I wish I had thought of that witty name. I have no hesitation in agreeing to their proposal. The work required to rebrand the game and loading screen is minimal. Within just a few hours of receiving their letter I complete the work to alter the game and loading screen, copy it onto a new cassette tape and post it back to them. I am encouraged that the software publisher appears to be taking my game seriously.

More good news arrives with an invitation to attend a job interview at the local department store. On the day of the interview, a gentleman called Mr Jenkins greets and escorts me to a vast open storage room, deep within the bowels of the store. In the centre of the room is a plain table and two chairs. The lighting is low and the scene is amusingly reminiscent to an integration scene from a gangster movie. Thankfully, the mood is relaxed and Mr Jenkins is a genial gentleman who quickly puts me at ease. Despite being my first ever job interview I answer his questions with ease and to the best of my abilities. Mr Jenkins is quick to comment on my apparent enthusiasm for computers, software and technology in general. The interview lasts for about an hour and I conclude by offering Mr Jenkins a look at my college credentials and certificates.

A few days later, Mr Jenkins telephones and invites me to accept the position of Computer Sales Person within the department store. Delighted, I promptly accept the post.

On arrival of my fist day in my new job, I am greeted warmly, particularly by two elderly female staff members, who, in the absence of a permanent and dedicated computer sales person have struggled to provide temporary cover for the post. It is clear from their enthusiasm of my arrival that they had found it difficult to work in that particular department and are pleased that they will not have to work there anymore. I am not surprised or put off by their reaction at all. Unfortunately, at this point in time, computers and software are typically a male pursuit. My college computer classes had been solely populated by males and you rarely see any females browsing the software sections of computer shops and department stores on the busy weekends.

The stores' computer department is huge. I am thrilled that I will now be responsible for its successful day to day operation. There are huge, impressive displays of the latest 8-bit and 16-bit computers for customers to play with. There are long shelves filled with hundreds of games, sorted by computer make and model. And there is also a decent sized section for computer and games magazines. Mine! All mine!

An interesting aspect of the department is the electronic point of sale system (EPOS), which features a digital laser pen reader connected to every cash register. This store is the first in the city to use an EPOS system and it is my first exposure to this interesting technology. When a customer is ready to pay for their items the sales person scans each item by gently dragging the digital laser pen along the barcode printed on the item's packaging. The information is then processed by computers and is primarily used for calculating the total value of each sale and well as pricing and stock control. Maths had never been my strongest subject and here once again are computers saving the day.

During the regular week days, the computer department only sees a steady stream of customers. Although, trade noticeably picks up after schools have finished for the day. Children are easily the biggest demographic of computer and software sales so it is unsurprising that the computer department is less busy during the core business hours. On the weekend however, the situation is far different. From the moment the store opens right up until the moment it closes, the computer department is an incredible hive of hyperactivity. Children and sometimes adults from all over the city descend to spend their money on the latest games for their home computer.

Occasionally, some clueless and ill prepared parents arrive wanting some much needed advice on which computer to buy for their child. As ever, there are only two real options, the Commodore 64 and Sinclair ZX Spectrum. There is also the Amstrad CPC464, which includes a built in cassette tape player and separate monitor, but I am not impressed by its internal architecture. With a semi unbiased epitome of professionalism I attempt to describe the merits of all computers fairly, but ultimately the ZX always reaps the benefit of my zeal.

By the time the store closes on a Saturday evening, the computer department looks as if it has been the target of a nuclear strike. The computer displays are swathed by sticky finger prints, the once alphabetised software is haphazardly abandoned anywhere and everywhere. And the neatly stacked computer and games magazines are mostly on the floor.

Each Monday morning, once I finish cleaning the mess from Saturday's onslaught, I review the hardware and software stock order that the EPOS computer generates. Against each entry, I have to agree or disagree with the proposal to order each item by writing a tick or a cross. In the instances where I place a cross I have to manually adjust the reorder value that had been suggested by the EPOS computer. One of the many benefits of using an EPOS system is that the computer provides you with a stock order based on previous sales and trends. It sounds good in theory, but what the EPOS computer cannot do is anticipate future sales. I spend a lot of time reading magazines and chatting to customers regularly. I can sense the vibe of the computer buying public. All the EPOS computer can do is see historical numbers.

One day, I read in a computer magazine that Amstrad are about to drop the price of their popular business computer the PCW 8512. When it was originally launched, the cost of a PCW system was under 25% of the cost of almost all IBM-compatible PC systems in the UK. As a result, Amstrad's PCW has become very popular in the home and small office markets, both in the UK and in Europe. The sales in my computer department have been steady, but not great. I learn that Amstrad are about to drop the price of this model in order to concentrate on their latest computer the PCW1512. I have a feeling that demand will significantly increase for the aging PCW 8512 at a new lower price so I amend the sales order from 1 unit to 6. When Mr Jenkins later learns what I have done he is understandably concerned that we could be stuck with a lot of aging stock. I explain about the impending price drop and that I genuinely believe the demand will suddenly increase. Nevertheless, he explains that I should have discussed it with him first and that he will have to inform the store manager of the situation. I am not at all concerned and within just a few weeks my actions are vindicated when I do in fact sell all six Amstrad PCW 8512s. In fact, the demand for the computer at the lower price is so great that other branches of the store throughout the country are telephoning me to request transfers from my precious stock. The swines!

Before leaving the house for work one morning, the postman delivers what is possibly the most wonderful package a teenage geek can receive. The package has been sent from the software company that are releasing my ZX Spectrum game and inside are two copies of my game complete with the finished cassette box and inlay artwork. Included with the two cassettes is a brief note which, explains that this is what my game will look like on the shelves and displays of computer shops up and down the country. This is the first opportunity that I have been given to review the artwork on the cassette inlay. It's okay, but nothing special. The thrill for me is seeing my name printed on the inside of the cassette box inlay. Thankfully, Top Ten Games spell my name correctly. Hallelujah.

One Monday morning, whilst meticulously scrutinising the EPOS stock order, I glance upon the accompanying news bulletin, which describes the week's forthcoming software releases. Buried, deep within the lines of text is an entry, which almost causes my heart to skip a beat with excitement. The line reads, 'Snookered by Top Ten Games'. Amusingly, the EPOS system is unconsciously alerting the author of this software that the game is new and now available to be ordered. The EPOS recommends that I should order four units, which is the standard value for any new software. Of course my natural instinct is to increase this value to a much higher figure such as one thousand, but common sense prevails and I simply do what I always do when I agree with the EPOS system, which is to place a tick next the entry. On this occasion I do so with a big smile

Later that week, when the computer and software delivery finally arrives, I tear open the packaging with a fevered frenzy in search of my creation. Eventually, I find all four of my games, neatly packed amongst the other, lesser software. The day has finally arrived where my game will now go on sale for the first time and in a bizarre twist of strange fate I will have the honour of putting the stock on display on the software shelves. The moment is not lost on me and I do what I always do when the universe delivers such curious happenstances, which is to smile wryly and shrug my shoulders in resignation to the higher, unbeknownst forces. With my game taking an unfair prime position amongst the ZX Spectrum software displays, it is inevitable that I will eventually be selling my own game to a customer. I am particularly looking forward to the day when this will happen.

Another interesting stock delivery arrives at the store this week, namely the new Commodore Amiga 16-bit computer. Intended as a logical replacement for the aging 8-bit Commodore 64 computer, the new Commodore Amiga will go head to head with Atari's 16-bit offering the Atari ST, which was released two years earlier. The computer media interest in the Commodore Amiga is big, mostly because of the impressive technical specifications, which include a Motorola 68000 microprocessor running at 7.15909 MHz, 512K RAM, four sound channels, and a built in floppy disk drive. The price tag on this impressive new machine is £599. Like the Atari ST, the Amiga is a big crowd puller and the display model frequently attracts huge swells of people clambering to see and play with the computer. By comparison, the popularity of the aging 8-bit computers on display, namely the Commodore 64, ZX Spectrum and Amstrad CPC464 are now starting to diminish.

The 8-bit market can no longer rely upon it's exclusivity of the market place. There are at least two new heavyweights on the scene with the promise of more 16-bit computers in the near future. The new machines are, bigger, faster, and can process more complex graphics and sound than their computing forefathers. The 8-bit market will have to do something innovative or simply roll over and allow the natural evolution of progression to take place.

Eventually, the day arrives when a customer walks up to the computer department sales counter and hands me a software box and some cash. The software is my game "Snookered". My initial instinct is to shake the customer's hand and congratulate him on his sensible selection. I want to boast that as author of the game I can personally vouch for the fun he was going to enjoy through his purchase. In fear of alienating my sole customer to date or even scaring him out of the store before I can complete the sale, I fight hard to suppress the urge. Once again I smile inanely at the ridiculousness of the situation and simply thank the customer for his custom, blissfully unaware that he has just been served by the author of his software purchase.

Within a few weeks of my game being released, the computer magazines begin to review my game. It is quite a thrill to see my game feature in all my favourite computer magazines, such as Crash and Your Sinclair. My humble little game is now sharing editorial space alongside the biggest and best releases from the major software publishers. Sadly, the reviews of my game are mixed. Some reviewers like the game, some do not. The general consensus is that Snookered is an average game at best. The reviews do not concern me too much. Of course it would be useful to receive glowing reviews, which will help drive sales, but I am not deluded. Whilst I consider my game to be worthy of a commercial release, it does not offer the player anything ground breaking. I feel the retail price of £1.99 is reasonable for what the game offers.

After a few short months employed as a computer sales person, the computer department manager Mr Jenkins forewarns me that through no fault of my own, sales are in decline. The combined monthly sales of computers and software are not meeting the store's projected targets. Mr Jenkins explains that since the release of dedicated video games consoles, such as the Nintendo NES and the Sega Master System, both of which the store does not sell, sales have suffered. If the situation does not improve then the store may have to consider reducing my role to part time or worse still laying me off. The revelation is a disappointing shock. I adore working in the computer department. It clearly is not a role that offers me a long term career, but for now, it provides me with a much needed income and affords me a level of access to the latest computers and software. Despite the disappointing news, I'm hopeful the sales of my first game will generate enough income and interest to facilitate the next stage of my career in computers.

Whatever that may be.

Chapter 7
Livin' On A Prayer
(or Chapter 00000111 for geeks)

1988 – NASA has resumed their Space Shuttle programme following the grounding after the truly terrible Challenger disaster three years earlier. Meanwhile, Sega launch the Mega Drive in Japan, a 16bit cartridge based games console that will surely never take off?

Surprisingly, I don't live in a plush bachelor pad and there is no fancy car parked outside. Despite having authored a commercially released computer game, I'm still living with Mum. How can this be?

After six long months, I still have not received a single penny of royalties from the sales of my game. The kudos of being a published games author has long diminished and my brain craves a new form of serotonin in the form of hard cash.

Sadly, Mr Jenkins' previous forewarning of diminishing sales and the possibility of reduced working hours has been realised and we unfortunately depart company. I've learnt a great deal from my first job in the computer department and I am grateful to Mr Jenkins for the experience and his tutelage.

It is time to re-establish contact with the software publisher and respectfully remind them that it has been six months since my game has been on sale. It seems far longer. I pluck up the nerve to telephone the publisher and whilst the conversation is cordial, there doesn't seem to be any sense of urgency or commitment on their part, just a vague promise of some payment in several weeks.

Those weeks extend into months and despite several more calls and the occasional letter, I am still a penniless author, albeit a published one. My internal bullshit detector has reached critical levels and I am now certain that the publisher has no intentions of fulfilling their contractual obligations. It is time to seek professional help.

Sitting the in the Lawyers office at the age of eighteen by myself is daunting. The office is clad in oak coloured, leather furniture and there are wall to wall bookshelves, strewn with old, thick, musky books. The entire room exudes law.

The lawyer is sat behind her great desk and gazes at me intently from behind her petite spectacles, which are delicately balanced on the end of her tiny nose. I am hopeful that this legal professional will save the day and get my cash.

One of my greatest regrets is that I didn't keep a copy of the contract between myself and the software publisher. Over time, I had lost it. It had been such a dizzying pleasure to have received the contract in the first place that I should have had it framed and lovingly adorned it on my wall for all to see. Hell, I should have stapled a copy to Mrs Jones' wrinkled old face and screamed "Computers are not for me huh?"

I had been a fool.

This massive neglect has put me and the Lawyer in a difficult position. Instead of using the might of the law, armed with a legally biding contract, we are going into battle with just my faded memory of a contract's details.

I explain to the Lawyer that I firmly believe the contract states that my game will retail for £1.99 and that I will receive 10 pence for every game that is sold. This doesn't seem to be a great amount of money, but games marketed at this price usually sell tens of thousands of units. With many familiar high street stores selling home computers and software, occasionally some of the best titles even exceed sales of hundreds of thousands of units.

After I finish telling my tale of woe, the Lawyer briefly reviews her notes and suggests that she should telephone the publisher there and then to discuss the situation. I am impressed by her gumption and agree to the proposal.

I sit patiently and listen to the Lawyer introduce herself to the software publisher. She speaks in a firm, but polite manner and explains the reason for her call. She recounts the events and occasionally sounds a reaffirming acknowledgment as she listens to the publisher's response.

After about ten minutes the Lawyer tells the publisher that she will discuss their offer with her client and call back shortly with an answer. My mind immediately locks onto the word "offer" and I allow myself to start feeling optimistic about a positive and prompt conclusion to this lengthy chapter. Perhaps that plush bachelor pad isn't such a pipe dream after all.

I could not be more wrong.

It seems my memory of the contract is only partially correct. Whilst it is true that the game does retail at £1.99, I will only receive 10% of the profits and not the 10 pence per unit that I had mistakenly thought.

There's not much margin for profit in an item that retails for £1.99. There are production costs of the cassette tape, printed inlay and plastic box. Then there are the distribution costs of getting the item to the retailers. And finally, the lion's share of the margin is swallowed up by the mighty retailers. There is very little profit left after all this. Despite being the architect of this creation, it seems software authors reside at the bottom of the pecking order when it comes to payment.

The Lawyer explains that the publisher is offering a single flat fee of just £200 for my work. Without a copy of the contract, without evidence of their costs and profit margins, without detailed sales figures the cause seems hopeless. I could be locked in a very expensive and very prolonged legal case that could extend for months, if not years.

There is even worse news to come. Up until this point, my time with the Lawyer has been "free". The reason for this is because as I am now unemployed, I'm therefore entitled to something called "Legal Aid". This means that I can get professional help, sign a green form and the state will cover the legal fees.

However, if at any time a client receives funds through the resulting action of the legal aid work then they are liable to cover the lawyer's fees with those funds. My Lawyer explains that if I accept the offer of the £200 from the publisher then her time and work will easily equal £200. She's only met me for less than an hour and made a single ad-hoc telephone call. Clearly I'm in the wrong business.

That is it. In an instant, the painful realisation swept through me that those six long months of difficult coding at a lonely keyboard, whilst being brain washed by Scoundrel Days were all for nothing. No contract. No payment. No hope. No bachelor pad. Game over man, literally.

I thank the Lawyer for her efforts and advise her to formally decline the software publisher's offer. This is a battle that will not be won from a Lawyers office. I need to regroup, rethink and recharge my spirits for another day. I leave the Lawyers office felling down, but certainly not out.

A few days latter I decide to try and find out how many copies of my game have been sold. It is clear that Top Ten

Games are not going to freely give up this information, so somehow I will find another way.

Whilst working as a sales assistant at the department store I had on occasion needed to discuss some sales related activity with the store's computer buyer at head office. I decide to write to the gentleman and explain my situation and ask how many copies of my game this particular company has sold.

To my surprise, the computer buyer at head office is quick with his response and discloses their full sales figures for my game. Snookered had sold the grand total of 500 units throughout this company's nationwide stores.

Okay, so it is not a great figure by itself, but this particular department store is just one of many that have sold my game. When you consider all the other department stores, plus the thousands of independent retailers you very quickly have the potential to sell a shit load of software.

Unfortunately, writing to every software retailer in the country to request accurate sales figures for my game isn't going to be an easy task and there is no guarantee that the retailers will relinquish their private business data as easily as the first department store had. Why would they? There is no incentive for them to do so.

It will probably be easier to write to the national software distributors, which I understand there are only about a dozen, who in turn supply all the major department stores and independent retailers, but at this stage I do not know who or where these companies are.

For the moment, I conclude that the sales figures of just one major department store are sufficient to base an estimation on the overall sales figures and help me decide what my next steps should be.

At this stage, I'm not quite sure what to do next or in fact whether I should do anything at all. The lawyer has failed to find an acceptable solution and I'm just a teenager, fresh out of college and wet behind the years.

Armed with the sales figure of a single national department store, I decide I will let some time pass and carefully consider what to do next.

Chapter 8
Money For Nothing
(or Chapter 00001000 for geeks)

1989 – A British engineer and computer scientist Sir Tim Berners-Lee, writes a proposal for his vision of something called the World Wide Web. Meanwhile, Nintendo release an 8-bit hand held game console called the Game Boy in both Japan and America. Despite many other, technologically superior handheld consoles introduced during its lifetime, the Game Boy and later, the Game Boy colour are a tremendous success. Combined they experience unparallel success and sell 118.69 million units worldwide.

The ever present spectre of poverty has led me to a painful realisation that I need some form of payment for my game, any payment. I need closure on an episode, which should have been a glorious achievement in a young person's life, but instead is constantly nagging away at my sub consciousness.

After much sole searching and the swallowing of my teenage pride I decide to write to the publisher and ask them if their offer of £200 is still available. I explain that I do not want to appear greedy or ungrateful and that their offer seems a fair one. A little piece of my soul dies.

A few days later, I receive a letter from the publisher, which commends my sense of fairness and patronisingly hints at the importance of never being greedy. They also enclose a cheque for £200. It is a bittersweet moment. I am grateful for the money, but I feel cheated. I vow never to have any further contact with this publisher again.

The rapidly growing popularity of 16-bit home computers such as the Commodore Amiga and Atari ST is now significantly impacting the diminishing dominance of the 8-bit home computer industry. Model specific computer magazines in particular are beginning to see their readership figures decline as users dump their aging 8-bit computers for the new machines. In an effort to stop the migration (and also to retain their sales), the popular 8-bit magazines have started to include cassettes with free software struck to the front of their magazine covers. These new additions, affectionately labelled as 'Cover Tapes', provide users with older, previously released games and demos of new ones. They are an instant success.

Up until this point, the cover tapes exclusively feature software from the major publishers. I wonder if there is an opportunity to have my own software on these cover tapes? I decide to write to my favourite magazine, (the aptly titled Crash) and ask if they would like to include my previously released game, but perhaps under a different title. The reason for a new title is to avoid any potential legal issues with the previous software publisher. Without a copy of the contract, I am unsure whether I have legally signed away all my rights to the game. I carefully calculate that the software publisher will not cry foul because in order to do so they will need to show the contract that I have signed. That in turn, would allow me to pursue them for unpaid royalties. It s a win win situation for me.

A few days later, the magazine agrees to my proposal. With updated graphics and a new title, 'Snookered' is transmogrified back into its original name, which is 'Break Point'. I become the first "reader" to have their software included on a cover tape of Crash magazine. I receive a single payment of £250 and bask in the knowledge that my game will be played (and hopefully enjoyed) by a readership base of nearly 100,000.

Despite college, work, and legal wrangles, I have continued to write software throughout the years and now have quite a portfolio of utility programs and games. The majority of this software has never really seen the light of day beyond the confines of my bedroom. The cover tape deal with Crash magazine has been a timely distraction from the problems with Top Ten Games, but it also presented a potential opportunity to strike a further deal to release some of my other work. Top of my unpublished list was a game called Ultimate Warrior - a 3D Isometric style game, which had been a popular format years earlier with such classics as Knight Lore and Head Over Heels.

The Cover Tape wars between the popular computer magazines are still very ripe. They are all competing with each other to obtain the exclusive rights to demos and full games. Once again, I write to Crash magazine and send a copy of Ultimate Warrior with an invitation to consider it for their cover tape. I am not at all surprised to receive a response soon after accepting the game. It wasn't because I thought the game was ground breaking or anything like that, it's because the magazines really are engaged in a bitter battle with each other to get decent software.

Unlike the previous occasion, I don't want the regular £250 payment for the game. This time, I propose that I have free advertising within the magazine as payment for the game. Despite my failed attempt some years earlier to sell Break Point by mail order through the same magazine, I want to try and revisit the concept and kick start a mail order software business with the many games and utilities that now make up my portfolio. Crash magazine agree to the deal and offers me a half page advertisement in the magazine. I am thrilled.

In order to take full advantage of this great opportunity I will dispense with the usual format of a loading screen for my cover tape game and instead I will add an advertisement for some of my other software. So whilst the user is sitting patiently for my game to load, instead of seeing a loading screen, which represents the game they are about to play, they will see an advertisement for my other games and utilities. This is in addition to the half page advertisement promised by Crash.

A few days after the Crash magazine with my game and advert are published; I sit waiting patiently at the top of my stairs, observing the front door and letterbox below to see what level of response the postman will bring. My abortive attempt several years earlier to sell software by mail order had been an utter disaster. A tiny eighth page advert had cost me £200. Now I was about to reap the benefits of a much larger advert worth about £1000, backed by the clever advertisement on the loading screen to my game. I have no way to predict the outcome of this double whammy marketing initiative.

When the postman finally arrives, nothing can prepare me for what happens next. The postman pushes an incredible amount of letters through my letterbox, and a few moments latter he pushes another massive bunch through, then another. Soon, the floor area underneath the letterbox has evolved into a small mountain of mail in various shapes and colours, all of which contain a cheque and an order for my software. The sight is incredible. I'm sat open mouthed and look down at the colourful mound and chuckle at my good fortune. The problems with Top Ten Games had soured my experience of the industry. The mail mountain before me has gone some way to restabilising my faith.

The next few weeks are busy, very busy. Similar to the illegal games copying service I had provided whilst as a child in school, once again I am copying software onto blank cassette and selling them. Only this time the software is mine and the business is 100% legitimate. Fortunately, I have already sourced and obtained a good supply of blank cassettes and padded envelopes and soon

I have developed an efficient production line where the orders are opened and processed. A cassette with the correct software is placed into a padded envelope and then later in the day I take the whole batch to the local post office for sending.

Each day, the postman continues creating a mountain of mail at the foot of my letterbox and each day I methodically process the orders as fast as was possible. The bank account swells and my twin cassette desk sweats under the strain of all the copying. This mini industry is being served by a grand workforce of one person, me.

Up to this point, the work as been barely manageable, the orders have been steady and I had the foresight to ensure decent levels of stock in the form of blank cassettes and padded envelopes. The hardest part is the copying. There is no quick way to produce a game on cassette. The entire manufacturing process to produce just one copy involves the following process: Insert the master cassette tape in deck one and insert the blank cassette tape in deck two. Press play on deck one. Press record on deck two. After five minutes, turn over the master cassette tape in deck one and turn over the now semi blank cassette tape in deck two, Press play on deck one. Press record on deck two. The entire copying process takes about 5-10 minutes (depending on the software) per cassette. The only way to speed up the process would be to buy an additional stereo unit with twin cassette desks, but this would cost about £200.

Very soon, I find myself trapped in an endless routine of hard work and laborious production, from which there seems to be no escape. Once the postman delivers his usual mail mountain, what was once a joy has now become a tedious task of opening and sorting the orders, followed by the continual copying of cassettes. All of which is topped off with the daily journey to the post office.

After about six weeks, the orders mercifully start to diminish. It has been a rewarding, but also exhausting experience. I have finally achieved my goal of running a modest mail order software business and have generated a lot of revenue. For the most part, it has been a lot of fun.

Crash magazine wants to know if I have any more gems to send their way and we briefly discuss the possibility of releasing Snookered II as a cover tape with an entirely new question base. Such a deal will allow me to continue with my mail order business, but I am now unconvinced about the continued viability of the 8-bit computer and software market. Some of the major software companies have stopped publishing software for the 8-bit computers and the readership figures of the 8-bit magazines, which had once been 100,000 were now down to between 20,000 to 30,000 per month. All the signs suggest that the decade long reign of the 8-bit computer market is on a very steep decline in favour of the new 16-bit computers.

I consider myself fortunate to have witnessed and experienced many aspects of the 8-bit industry. It has been an incredible journey of discovery and I am grateful to have enjoyed the many opportunities that have come my way either through design or cosmic intervention. After much soul searching I decline Crash magazine's offer to produce and release any more ZX Spectrum software. My heart simply is not in it any more. I am no longer passionate about the 8-bit market. I have achieved and experienced more than most and for that I will be forever grateful.

It is the last time I will ever write a computer program.

Chapter 9
Ashes To Ashes
(or Chapter 00001001 for geeks)

1990 – Microsoft Windows version 3.0 is released and is the first Microsoft Windows version to achieve broad commercial success, selling 2 million copies in the first six months. It features improvements to the user interface and to multitasking capabilities. Meanwhile, Nintendo releases its second gaming console called the Super Nintendo, which goes on to become the best selling 16-bit console. This is despite its relatively late start and fierce competition from Sega's Mega Drive console.

All good things must come to an end and the 8-bit home computer revolution is no exception to this maxim.

With the introduction of the 16-bit heavyweights a few years earlier it is a foregone conclusion that the death of 8-bit will eventually come to pass. The lure of the mighty Atari ST and Commodore Amiga are simply too alluring for the computer owning fraternity to dismiss and pass by. The attempt by the computer media to reinvigorate declining sales through cover tapes has merely delayed the inevitable conclusion of the 8-bit era, although they deserve some credit for their efforts.

Like me, even the die hard 8-bit aficionados who impassionedly hold onto their 8-bit boxes of bliss must eventually concede to the unstoppable evolution of this technology. Together, the superior specifications of the Atari ST and Commodore Amiga have contributed to the end of this once thriving industry. The king is dead. Long live the king.

Surprisingly, the reign of the new 16-bit super heroes is fleeting and does not enjoy the impressive longevity of their 8-bit forefathers. Despite their advanced architecture, the Atari ST and Commodore Amiga, as indeed all the many makes and models before them, all suffer from a single, significant drawback. They are all completely and utterly incompatible with each other. It is not just the operating system or software; it is also the architecture. Everyone is doing "their own thing". Even the various expansion ports on each machine all employ their own custom sockets and connectors. There is simply no collaboration between the manufacturers and the end user suffers as a consequence through incompatibility and inflated prices. The situation seems hopeless. So its little wonder that enthusiasts have tired of the situation and embrace the introduction of a simpler, cheaper and more consistent approach.

The first saviour (or destroyer, depending on your view) is the introduction of a standardised and easily expandable hardware platform coupled with a user friendly operating system. I am of course referring to the modern PC running Microsoft Windows.

IBM compatible PCs (as they were initially known) have existed for some time, but up until this point, the hardware has been modest. With significant advances in computer and hardware technology the typical specification now includes at least a 16Mhz 386SX processor, a 30MB hard drive, a CD-ROM drive, a 1.44MB 3.5-inch floppy drive, a 640x480 video output, eight note sound card, serial, parallel, MIDI and game ports, a two-button mouse and an incredible 2MB of RAM. I can not imagine a situation where anyone would need more RAM than that, ever.

The specifications of the 8-bit and 16-bit home computers are pitiful compared to these modern standards. Intriguingly, 'Moore's Law' now appears conceivable. The law states that the power of a microprocessor doubles every 18 months and it becomes easier to simply dispose of the PC than to upgrade or repair it.

Another previously off putting reason why IBM compatibles were previously unappealing to the mass market was the non user friendly operating system called MS-DOS (Microsoft Disk Operating System). This command-line interface (CLI) forced the user to interact with the computer by entering commands in the form of a line of text (a command line). This cumbersome approach meant the user needed to possess in-depth knowledge of MS-DOS commands in order to perform basic operations. Clearly a simpler solution is needed.

Microsoft Windows 3.0 runs as an intuitive, Graphical User Interface (GUI) running on top of the complicated

MS-DOS. The introduction of a Windows based system has really changed everything. With simple clicks on user friendly icons, even the Luddite members of your family can achieve most computing tasks, but without the need for specialist knowledge.

Aside form the advancements and standardisation of the desktop PC, the second possible contributing factor towards the decline of the 8-bt and 16-bit home computer industry is the introduction of dedicated gaming consoles. It is generally accepted that the main use of home computers is to play games. The vast sales of gaming software over the sales of application and utility based software confirm this belief. Both Nintendo and Sega had previously enjoyed some success with their third generation video game consoles such as the Nintendo Entertainment System and the Sega Master System. The decline of the home computer market has been further expedited with the release of the Super Nintendo Entertainment System (SNES) and the Sega Mega Drive. Other notable game consoles are the hugely underrated NEC TurboGrafx-16 and SNK Neo Geo.

Ironically, this reverse in trend from home computers to gaming consoles has mirrored the great video game crash of 1983. Prior to that crash, early gaming consoles such as the Atari 2600 and Magnavox Odyssey ruled supreme until the growing number of home computer users caused consumers and retailers to lose faith and interest in video game consoles. Many video game console companies filed for bankruptcy, or moved into other industries.

So in conclusion, I don't believe a single reason can be attributed to the demise of the 8-bit and 16-bit home computer industries. My belief is that the timely evolution of modern PC coupled with consumer demand for cheaper, dedicated video games consoles has brought the beginning of the end to this once innovative decade.

My only hope is that the pioneering spirit of the great innovators from this period are not lost to the annals of time and that they will find new opportunities in the new order.

```
10 PRINT "Thank you for playing."
20 GOTO 10
RUN
```

Epilogue

2014 – The World is starting to recover from the recent economic downturn in growth, with many European countries still suffering the effects of a European sovereign debt crisis. Much of the Middle East continues to squabble with each other and Argentina is embarrassingly and incredulously still bleating on about the Falkland Islands to anyone that will listen (nobody is). On the technology front, Microsoft's Windows continue their seemingly unassailable domination as the most popular PC operating system. Meanwhile Google's Android system has overtaken Apple as the most popular Smart Phone operating system.

As I sit at my laptop and complete this final chapter of this book, I continue to be in awe of the advanced architecture and specification of my laptop and other such computing devices.

The super fast processor speeds, the large memory size, the vast hard drive capacity, even the simple act of having a built in display, all these individual elements are so far ahead of their humble 8-bit forefathers of yesteryear.

And what do most users do with this amazing technology? We fritter it away on banal trivialities such as Facebook, Twitter and Angry Birds. What a shame.

Understandably, it's difficult for today's youth to understand the significance of the technology they so readily use and enjoy today. Notebooks, gaming consoles, smart phones, high speed Internet access are all enthusiastically utilised and yet typically undervalued. Unless you were a part of this emerging technology in the '80s you won't have experienced the vibe of its ascendance and appreciate its path of evolution. But not me. I treasured every ground breaking moment that has lead us to the advances that we enjoy today. I wish I could claim to have played some significant role in that journey, but the reality is that I just wrote a few simple programs, which through various happy accidents received a small audience. I was just a very tiny eighties guppy in a very big technological pond.

I will concede to the belief that perhaps today's youth are experiencing a type of ground-breaking period. Advancements in mobile technology, such as smart phones and tablets are accelerating at a seemingly unabated pace. The ability to instantly share your daily musings and photos through social media has radically changed the way people communicate, not just with family and friends, but with strangers also. But no matter how hard you attempt to justify the technological merits of any particular decade, you will never truly match the spirit and vibe that were created in the '80s. It really was a unique and pioneering decade of advancement.

As for the future, I have long stopped trying to predict the next big thing. I continue to be fascinated by the latest developments and I still get excited when a new life enhancing piece of technology is released for the first time. My ever changing choice of smart phone is testimony to this fact.

One technological development that has caught both my imagination and interest is the new range of small, budget computers aimed at the educational and hobbyist markets and intended to encourage people to learn programming. The British designed Raspberry Pi is about the size of a credit card and built around the Arm chip that can be found in the vast majority of mobile phones. The operating system is based upon a version of the Linux operating system and uses SD cards as its storage medium. The computer also comes in two varieties - with and without a networking connector.

The new generation of small, low cost computers appears to have caught the imagination of Google's chairman Eric Schmidt. In a speech in early 2012 , Mr Schmidt paid tribute to the UK's "Great Computing Heritage", but warned the UK risked "losing a generation" due to the current focus which is learning how to use software rather than learning how to make software. Mr Schmidt paid tribute to the innovations of the 8-bit era, specifically the introduction of the BBC Micro into schools during the early '80s and donated funds to train 100 teachers and supply teaching aids such as the Raspberry PI. Whether these new innovations and incentives recapture the spirit and success of their early eighties forefathers remains to be seen, but certainly the efforts of these organisations are a positive step in the right direction.

As for myself, over the years, my love of technology has never diminished. Ever since I received my humble Sinclair ZX81 in Christmas 1983 I have continued to own, use and enjoy a computer in some form or another almost every day. For decades, I have used computers and technology extensively in various Information Technology roles for some familiar organisations including: British Telecom, Virgin Media, and ITV.

At the time of writing this book, I work as an Information Technology Service Management (ITSM) specialist in Wales' National Health Service, where my main duties are to provide ITSM consultancy for the largest Microsoft Active Directory and Exchange Server installation in the country. It's a role I'm hugely proud of and which I never take it for granted. Mother of course, still doesn't quite understand exactly what I do and labels my job simply as "computers".

Outside of work, for a number of years I became interested in web site design and HTML. I successfully designed and managed two popular websites, which between them received over one million visitors. The resulting traffic generated enough income using click-through advertising to entirely fund the operation.

My quest for learning has also remained with me over the decades. Today, I'm the proud holder of the Information Technology Service Management ITIL version 2 and 3 qualifications and well as a CompTia A+ Core Hardware & Operating Software (OS) Technologies certification.

When I consider Mrs Jones' original and merciless snub, I like to think I have attained my modest lot in life **despite her** rejection, when in fact, it should have been **because of her** tutelage.

When I reflect on the wonderful 80's I'm reminded about three things.

1. You can never have enough RAM.

2. I still know all the words to all the songs on the album Scoundrel Days.

3. Mrs Nicola Jones was so wrong.

Glossary

Here are some explanations of some of the terms that have featured in this book.

8-Bit

An 8-bit computer that is capable of transferring 8 bits of data at a time.

16-Bit

A 16-bit computer that is capable of transferring 16 bits of data at a time.

Audio Cassette Tape

See Cassette.

Bit

Abbreviation for binary digit, the smallest unit of information on a computer or storage. A single bit can hold only one of two values: 0 or 1.

Byte

Abbreviation for binary term, a unit of information on a computer or storage capable of holding a single character. On almost all computers, a byte is equal to 8 bits.

Cassette

The Compact Cassette, also called audio cassette, cassette tape, cassette, or simply tape, is a magnetic tape sound recording format. It was designed originally for dictation and ultimately used for music and computer software.

Console

A Console is a dedicated entertainment computer system, which is typically connected to a conventional television set and used mostly to play video games.

Cover Tape

An audio cassette, containing software, usually full versions of previously released games and limited demos of new games, attached to the front of a magazine as a gift.

Graphic

A graphic is a computer generated image and capable of being displayed on the screen.

GUI

Abbreviation for a graphical user interface (pronounced gooey) is a type of user interface that allows users to interact with computers with intuitive images rather than specialised text commands.

Hardware

The physical electronic components of a computer.

Listing

A listing or program listing is a printed list of lines of computer code commonly used in '80s computer enthusiast books and magazines.

Loading Screen

Loading screens are similar in concept to a book cover and used to distract from the length of time that a program takes to load from cassette tape.

Nicola Jones

A very spiteful woman.

Processor

The Central Processing Unit (CPU) is responsible for interpreting and executing most of the commands from the computer's hardware and software. The CPU could be considered the 'brains' of the computer.

RAM

RAM, short for Random Access Memory is the short storage area for your PC. Often just called memory or system memory RAM is just an electromagnetic storage that loses all its data once the power has been removed. You can never have enough RAM.

Software

Software is a general term for the various kinds of programs used to operate computers and related devices.

Thank you

Dear valued Reader, thank you for reading my book. Regardless of how you came across this title, whether it was through an online purchase, in a book store or maybe you even offered a few pennies and rescued it from the indignity of a jumble/garage sale, your interest and support is gratefully acknowledged and sincerely appreciated.

If you enjoyed this book, please tell others. Authors are dependant on good reviews and the interest created by your positive vibe could make the difference between me eating steak or spam for my dinner tonight. Imagine the horror!

Most online marketplaces welcome reviews from their customers; maybe you could take a few moments from your daily schedule to leave a few comments. Even if it doesn't persuade others to emulate your courageous plunge, it will let me know that you are out there and that this particular book wasn't in vain.

Here's hoping we connect once again in book land.

Best wishes.

Steven.
Swansea, Wales.

12833214R00058

Printed in Poland
by Amazon Fulfillment
Poland Sp. z o.o., Wrocław